GARY GOLIO   ILLUSTRATED BY ANDREA D'AQUINO

SILENCE SOUNDS SIMPLE

A DAY IN THE LIFE OF JOHN CAGE

CALKINS CREEK
AN IMPRINT OF ASTRA BOOKS FOR YOUNG READERS
New York

THERE IS NO SUCH THING AS
AN EMPTY SPACE OR AN EMPTY TIME,
THERE IS ALWAYS SOMETHING TO SEE,
SOMETHING TO HEAR.

—John Cage

OVERTURE
john
cage
sound
sorcerer

made music with

screws   bolts   rubber bands

STUCK in piano strings
STUCK in your mind.

he'd have you
sit and listen
for several   minutes
to 12 radios playing

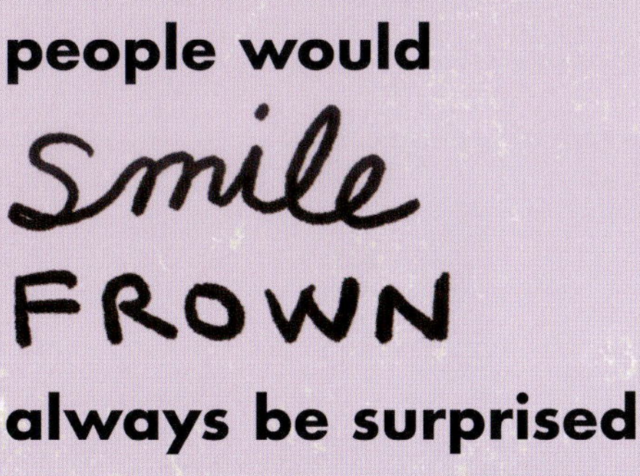

people would

smile **FROWN**

always be surprised

he played

a toy piano   onstage   in his suit

he
made you think.
?

thinking newly
freshly changes
your mind

changes
you

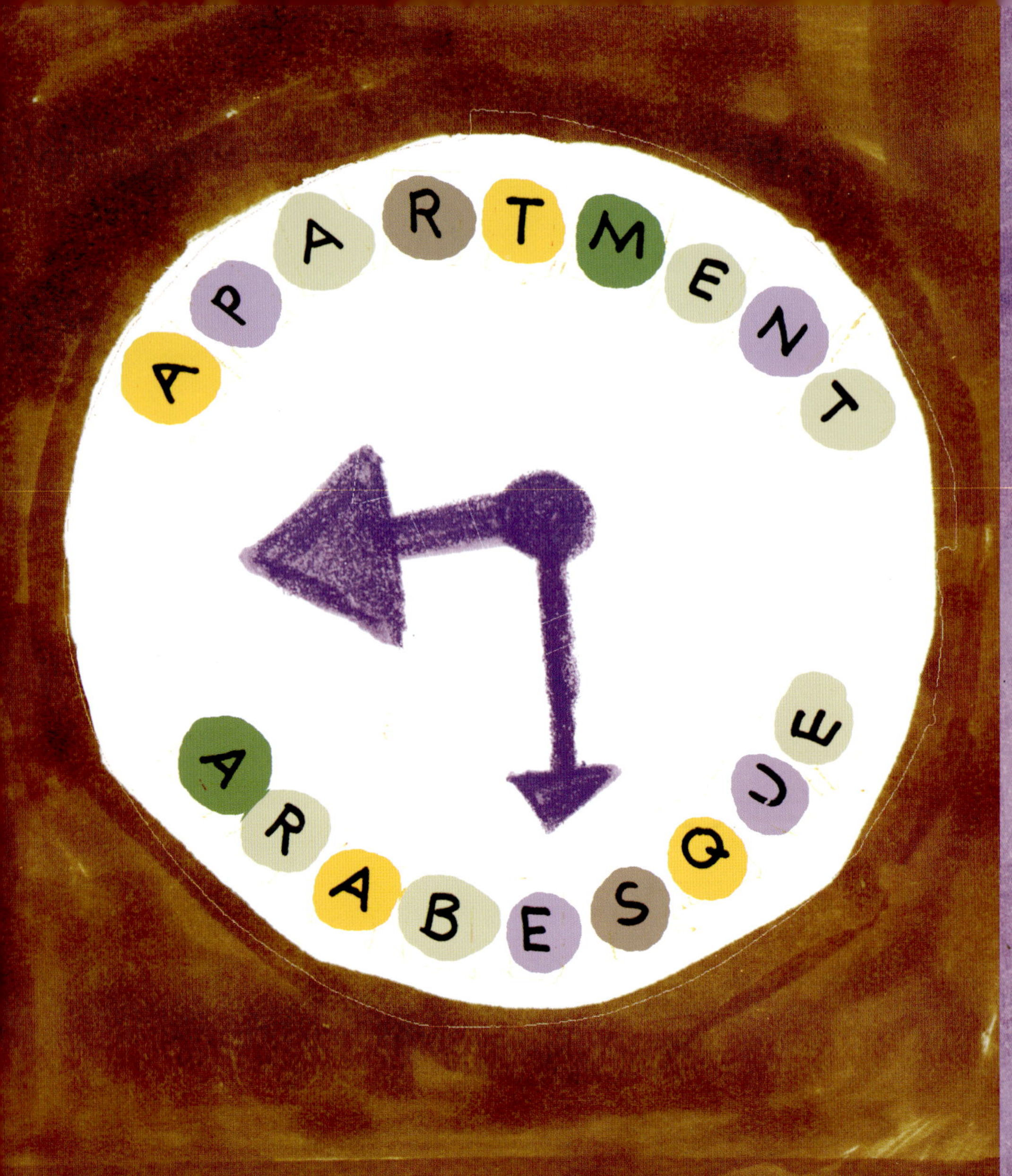
APARTMENT
ARABESQUE

the (((CLICK))) of a clock
the :RING: of a bell
a YAWN a groan
a GIGGLE

ha!

slippers *scuffing* on the old wooden floor

the **CLINK** of a spoon in a cup of tea

water **WHOOSHING** from a faucet

the **sizzle** of a pot on the stove

LAUGHTER from the
radio noises voices
singing in Spanish
humming hello to

an open chessboard
knight to rook
WHIZZ a windup bird
goes whirring

the meow of a cat
a purr
a scratch on the door
an itch in the ear

hello
hmmm

plants   high   lowest
long leaves flapping
barefoot feet
touch   TICKLE   tapping

HISSES of steam from the
heat pipes
a gust of wind
creaking CREEKY window glass

a musical good
bye from old friend Merce
the (((CLICK))) of the door
closing latching

silence
or is it?

STREET

stepping outside the
air filled with

sounds
abound

BEEPING horns
screeching brakes
clicking heels on the
sidewalk   stairs   shuffling

SERENADE

yawning YELLING
subway wheels
squeal as
doors slide wide

rumble
CLANK
whish
we're off!

I N T E R
what's
between the
notes and noises
peep
sounds within silence
silence in noise
music in both
life within all
zzz

L U D E
?
everything
needs
the otherthing
to give it life
after all
is there
sound without silence
silence without sound?

WOODS WALTZ

all over the world
thousands of people
listen
to John's concerts yet
here he is
now
alone
in a woods
on the ground
gently
lifting out a
mushroom
covered in dirt
holding it up
to the light
like a diamond
a symphony
as it makes music
only it can make

who's to say
that mushroom
spores
hitting the ground
don't make a sound

the only question
is
who's listening?

open your ears
open your mind
open to life
all around you

YOU ARE
the music
the noise
the silence

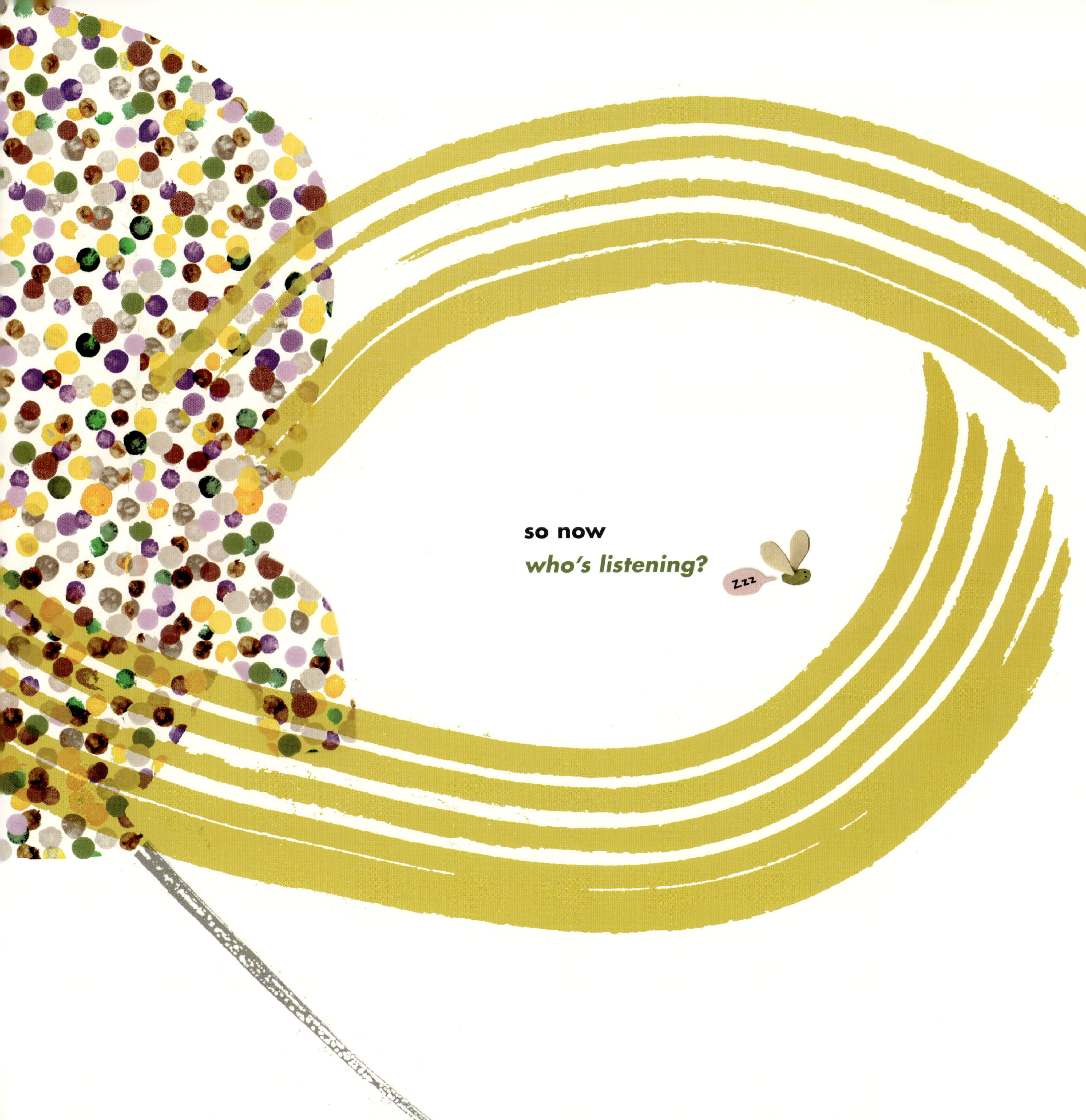

so now
who's listening?
zzz

JOHN CAGE
Mischief Maker and Mushroom Hunter

John Milton Cage Jr. was born and grew up in sunny Los Angeles, California. A bright and curious only child, he began taking piano lessons in the fourth grade and always enjoyed writing. John's mother wrote for a city newspaper and ran her own arts-and-crafts store. John's father was a gifted inventor (he even designed an early submarine!), and once told his son that "if someone says 'can't,' that shows you what to do."

First in his high school graduating class at age sixteen, John gave a prizewinning speech at the Hollywood Bowl (a famous outdoor theater) asking Americans to be "hushed and silent" and "hear what other people think"—rather than telling them what to believe.

John then went on to college hoping to become a writer. In the library one day, he was "shocked" to see all one hundred of his classmates reading the same book. So he pulled one off the shelves "by an author whose name began with Z," wrote his paper, and got the highest grade in the class. After that, John thought he'd learn more by traveling and studying on his own than by doing the same things as everyone else.

In Europe, he tried painting and writing poetry, but finally decided to devote his life to music. After studying with some trailblazing composers of the 1930s, John began doing some new and unusual work of his own. He wrote piano songs in ancient Greek, had people make music by hitting, shaking, or scraping all sorts of objects, and even created pieces using math equations. When asked to write something for dancers in a small theater with only a piano, he put screws, bolts, and rubber bands between the strings and turned a single instrument into an entire orchestra of strange and wonderful sounds!

Through his study of Zen Buddhism (a path of self-discovery), John brought more new ideas into his music: that every sound—like every living thing—has its own special identity; that each sound—like each person—is neither good nor bad; and that sound or silence cannot exist without the other. This led to him exploring electronic music, writing more pieces for dance, and staging "happenings" where many things took place onstage at the same time. For John, these events felt more like *life itself* than art shown in a museum or a piece of music performed in a concert hall. Such a performance was different from one moment to the next and could never be repeated.

Perhaps John's most famous piece of "music" is called *4'33"* (1952), where someone sitting at a piano starts a stopwatch and stays still for 4 minutes and 33 seconds while the audience listens to all the sounds around them. John's message was that *music is sound, happening all around us at every moment*, and that *paying attention to the noise of life* helps us appreciate "music" in a bigger way. Over the years, many music lovers told him that *4'33"* had changed their lives—and their minds.

John spent years composing music for his friend Merce Cunningham's dance company, each of them believing that movement and music could take place separately onstage to create something that each person would see and hear differently. John *trusted* the audience, rather than telling them how to think and feel. In this way, he gave more freedom to those who heard his music and watched Merce's dance, letting each speak for itself.

People who knew and met John describe a man with crinkly eyes who laughed a lot, shared his time and talents with others, and enjoyed both his life and his work. He influenced many artists, musicians, and people who read his books or essays, whether he was talking about mushrooms (his passion), chess (his pastime), or cooking (his pleasure). He rightfully wondered why we call one sound "music" and another "noise," and hoped, more than anything, to *change minds* (most of all his own!) rather than force his beliefs on others. He was a seeker exploring the unknown, inspired by endless curiosity, who was always willing to try and fail.

John examining a mushroom

Onstage, playing his toy piano

Silence Is

If you are curious, sit somewhere and listen—to your breathing, your heartbeat, and whatever sounds of life are taking place around you. If you sit in a fairly *quiet* place (a closed room, a closet, a car), perhaps at night, do you notice *the sound of silence*? It's real and it's unexpected, like a hum or whirr or the faint chirping of crickets. And ask yourself: What is it that lies between the sounds? What really *is* silence? John Cage believed it was *the absence of intended sounds*, which hints at the nature of noise and music. He also believed that true music is the sound of everything—our daily life, wherever we are—and that there's real value in taking time to listen, for it can *change your mind.*

I've had for a long time the desire to hear the mushroom itself, and that would be done with very fine technology, because they are dropping spores and those spores are hitting surfaces. There certainly is sound taking place.

—John Cage

Searching the woods with his mushroom basket

The Music of Mushrooms

When John Cage was a young man with very little money, he found mushrooms growing near his home, took out a book from the library to identify them (wild mushrooms can be poisonous!), and feasted for a week. John being John, his interest became a passion, and he devoted himself to studying—and *eating*—mushrooms.

John's interest in mushrooms lasted all his life. He wrote books about them, collected and sold them, taught college classes about them, and even led people on mushroom-hunting nature walks. John also founded the present-day New York Mycological (Mushroom) Society in New York City, and spent hundreds of hours in woods, parks, and forests all over the world looking for mushrooms. And while many people think of these marvelous fungi as simply *mold and dirt*, John believed they were worthy of our interest—not just as food, but as living things capable of their own music. He even famously predicted (see quote at left) that we would one day be able to hear those sounds for ourselves.

Recently, John's prediction came true, as exciting new technologies (using computers and sound synthesizers) allow researchers and musicians to *hear the music* of mushrooms. What may be more startling—and certainly would have made John smile—is that musicians have begun making music *with* mushrooms, in a sort of fungus-human symphony! To learn about and hear mushroom music itself, google "the secret sounds of mushrooms" or explore the link below.

And good mushroom-music-hunting!

kutx.org/features/the-secret-sounds-of-mushrooms/

It's a curious idea perhaps, but a mushroom grows for such a short time and if you happen to come across it when it's fresh it's like coming upon a sound which also lives a short time.

—John Cage

Bibliography

All the quotations in the book can be found in the following sources marked with an asterisk (*).

*Cage, John. *Silence: Lectures and Writings.* Middletown, CT: Wesleyan University Press, 1961.

*Cage, John, and Laura Kuhn. *The Selected Letters of John Cage.* Middletown, CT: Wesleyan University Press, 2016.

Gann, Kyle. *No Such Thing as Silence: John Cage's 4'33".* New Haven, CT: Yale University Press, 2010.

*Kostelanetz, Richard. *Conversing with Cage.* New York: Limelight Editions, 1988.

Larson, Kay. *Where the Heart Beats—John Cage, Zen Buddhism, and the Inner Life of Artists.* New York: Penguin, 2012.

*Ross, Alex. "Searching for Silence—John Cage's Art of Noise." Website issue of *The New Yorker Magazine*, September 27, 2010. newyorker.com/magazine/2010/10/04/searching-for-silence.

Wilson, Sally. "John Cage: The Mushroom Man." Website issue #29 of *The Plant Hunter*, May 26, 2016. theplanthunter.com.au/culture/john-cage.

**Water Walk*, 1960 (video): Watch this *unforgettable*—and seriously funny—music performance by John Cage, on national TV, using a bathtub, electric blender, rubber duckie, plastic fish, party popper, prepared piano, pressure cooker, glass with ice cubes, seltzer bottle, watering can, five radios, and a tape recorder. [You can go to YouTube.com or google "John Cage: Water Walk."] youtube.com/watch?v=gXOIkT1-QWY.

Acknowledgments

Much gratitude to Jennifer Baker and Caitlin Margaret Kelly of the David M. Rubenstein Rare Book and Manuscript Library at Duke University for their kind and gracious permission to use William Gedney's marvelous photos of John Cage. And sincere thanks to Andrea D'Aquino and her spunky Kat.

Picture Credits

Text copyright © 2026 by Gary Golio
Illustrations copyright © 2026 by Andrea D'Aquino
All rights reserved. Copying or digitizing this book for storage, display, or distribution in any other medium is strictly prohibited.

For information about permission to reproduce selections from this book, please contact permissions@astrapublishinghouse.com.

Calkins Creek
An imprint of Astra Books for Young Readers,
a division of Astra Publishing House
astrapublishinghouse.com
Printed in China

ISBN: 978-1-6626-8080-9 (hc)
ISBN: 978-1-6626-8079-3 (eBook)
Library of Congress Control Number: 2025944849

First edition

10 9 8 7 6 5 4 3 2 1

Design by Barbara Grzeslo and Michelle Mayhall
The text is set in Futura Std, Albus, and Adrianna.
The illustrations are monoprints with acrylic paint, oil pastel, cut paper, collage, and a wide variety of non-art supplies.
Illustrations published by arrangement with Debbie Bibo Agency.